Violet Roses

A Book of Blooms, Birds and Inspiration

KATHLEEN ELINOR

WestBow Press books may be ordered through booksellers or by contacting:

WestBow Press
A Division of Thomas Nelson & Zondervan
1663 Liberty Drive
Bloomington, IN 47403
www.westbowpress.com
844.714.3454

Written and Illustrated by Kathleen Elinor

Scripture taken from the New King James Version®. Copyright © 1982 by Thomas Nelson. Used by permission. All rights reserved.

ISBN: 978-1-6642-0419-5 (sc)
ISBN: 978-1-6642-0420-1 (e)

Library of Congress Control Number: 2020916740

Print information available on the last page.

WestBow Press rev. date: 09/21/2020

WESTBOW
P R E S S®
A DIVISION OF THOMAS NELSON
& ZONDERVAN

To Mom

Acknowledgments

I extend a gracious thanks and expression of sincere appreciation to botanical artists Pierre-Joseph Redoute and Susan Gaber, both my teachers from a distance of time and place but, teachers none the less. I have learned so much by observation of their skillful floral drawings and am blessed to have found them, learning flower botany, shape and structure. Thank you for the joy of drawing from the example of your Fine Art.

I also wish to acknowledge the photographers who through their talent and keen eye have enabled me to render the beauty of wildlife as artist and interpreter using the tools and medium of my craft.

VIOLET ROSES

This morning the roses blossomed not as I
had expected

Rather, they grew the color violet much like
looking to a purplish sky, the Heavens.

Love

The violet roses drew me in, their scent wafted through my garden

God's petals of delight to my eyes, new growth.

Joy

My senses took in their fragrance and I became a part of the sweet fresh scent.

Peace

Where will God take me today? To my garden of violet roses ever fresh, ever full, everlasting blossoms.

Patience

It is unusual to see a violet rose, a rare
blessing that I pick and treasure and call
my own.

Walking the path, I look about and see what
has always been there, precious, a gift from
above, a blossom in my garden.

Kindness

I will pick all that grow and as I pick still another sprouts so that as I give, I may give even more.

A bouquet brilliant with light held in my hand and given to my friend from the Friend from above, a growth in His Creation.

Goodness

How can I explain this phenomenon? Only to the violet sky do I look upward to find my answer.

Roses of violet a cherished amethyst, but, lovelier still for they are more rare than the amethyst.

Faithfulness

I remember when I planted the seeds
in the autumn when the coolness of the
air promised coming days of spring and
summer, of warmth and light and growth,
violet roses from seed, I am gratefully
pleased.

Gentleness

Pure violet, how it grows I cannot explain
and yet, it is there to take away times of
sorrow or difficulty, unexplained.

Full and plentiful they grow making for joy.

Temperance

I hear a melodic song, God's small birds have perched on the stems and brought for themselves glory on God's fragrant green branches.

Hope

How long will my bouquet last? A lifetime I am sure to bring morning glory to each new day of life.

Violet roses what a surprise, they were always in my garden once the seeds had been sown.

The spring showers came, then the sun did shine, even while the winds did blow as the seeds germinated in the ground below.

Bless

Each day I watched as God's hand laid bare
the shape that each flower would take. Each
shape He did form.

Believe

And today I see in the glorious garden a sea of violet roses for me and to you.

As I give we all have the seeds now,

Able to plant what God has created as His perfect plan.

Trust

The way that we plant, the way that we sow, the way that we care, are surely God's reward of flowers of violet.

Grace

Violet roses, how I smile at their color with joyful surprise.

They bloomed at just the right hour.

I could not have imagined nor planned the Heavenly Gift from God's own hand,

A harvest to give which God had intended as His Perfect Gift to me and to you.

Wisdom

Our Maker's hands from which all good things come.

Peace I leave with you, My peace I give to you… (John 14:27 NKJV)